LET'S PLAY SPORTS!

Soccer

by Thomas K. Adamson

BELLWETHER MEDIA • MINNEAPOLIS, MN

Note to Librarians, Teachers, and Parents:

Blastoff! Readers are carefully developed by literacy experts and combine standards-based content with developmentally appropriate text.

Level 1 provides the most support through repetition of high-frequency words, light text, predictable sentence patterns, and strong visual support.

Level 2 offers early readers a bit more challenge through varied simple sentences, increased text load, and less repetition of high-frequency words.

Level 3 advances early-fluent readers toward fluency through increased text and concept load, less reliance on visuals, longer sentences, and more literary language.

Level 4 builds reading stamina by providing more text per page, increased use of punctuation, greater variation in sentence patterns, and increasingly challenging vocabulary.

Level 5 encourages children to move from "learning to read" to "reading to learn" by providing even more text, varied writing styles, and less familiar topics.

Whichever book is right for your reader, Blastoff! Readers are the perfect books to build confidence and encourage a love of reading that will last a lifetime!

This edition first published in 2020 by Bellwether Media, Inc.

No part of this publication may be reproduced in whole or in part without written permission of the publisher. For information regarding permission, write to Bellwether Media, Inc., Attention: Permissions Department, 6012 Blue Circle Drive, Minnetonka, MN 55343.

Library of Congress Cataloging-in-Publication Data

Names: Adamson, Thomas K., 1970- author.
Title: Soccer / by Thomas K. Adamson.
Description: Minneapolis, MN : Bellwether Media, Inc., 2020. | Series: Blastoff! Readers : Let's play Sports! | Includes bibliographical references and index. | Audience: Ages: 5-8. | Audience: Grades: K-3.
Identifiers: LCCN 2018058483 (print) | LCCN 2019003047 (ebook) | ISBN 9781618915436 (ebook) | ISBN 9781644870020 (hardcover : alk. paper)
Subjects: LCSH: Soccer–Juvenile literature.
Classification: LCC GV943.25 (ebook) | LCC GV943.25 .A378 2020 (print) | DDC 796.334–dc23
LC record available at https://lccn.loc.gov/2018058483

Editor: Rebecca Sabelko   Designer: Andrea Schneider

Printed in the United States of America, North Mankato, MN.

Table of Contents

What Is Soccer?

Soccer is the most popular sport in the world! In most countries it is called football.

Soccer teams play on a large field.

soccer game in Brazil

Each team has 10 players and a **goalie**. Players kick the ball to pass and shoot.

goal

goalie

- forward

- La Liga and Argentina National Team

- Accomplishments:
  - FIFA World Player of the Year 5 times
  - Holds record for most goals scored in a calendar year: 91 in 2012
  - Won Spanish La Liga title 9 times

They try to kick the ball into the **goal**.

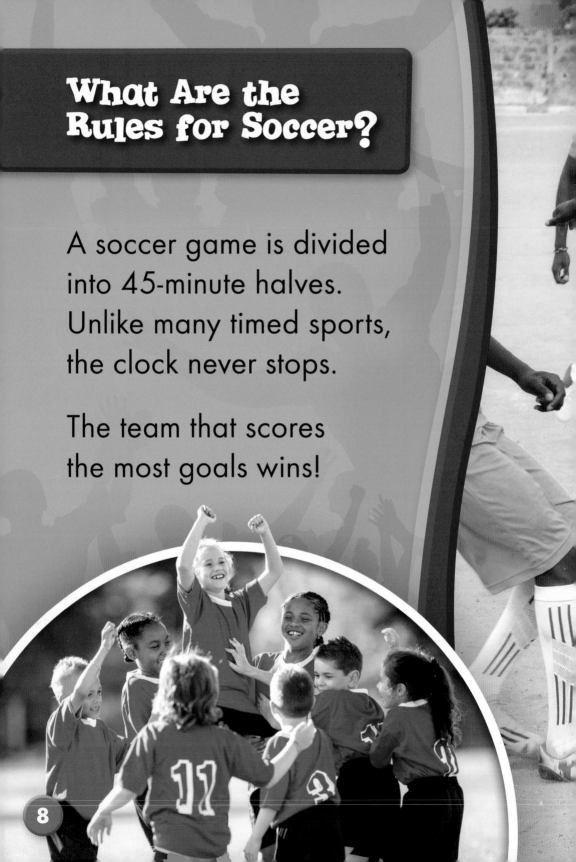

What Are the Rules for Soccer?

A soccer game is divided into 45-minute halves. Unlike many timed sports, the clock never stops.

The team that scores the most goals wins!

trapping the ball

Players use their feet, knees, or heads to pass the ball. They use their chests to **trap** the ball.

They cannot use their
hands or arms.

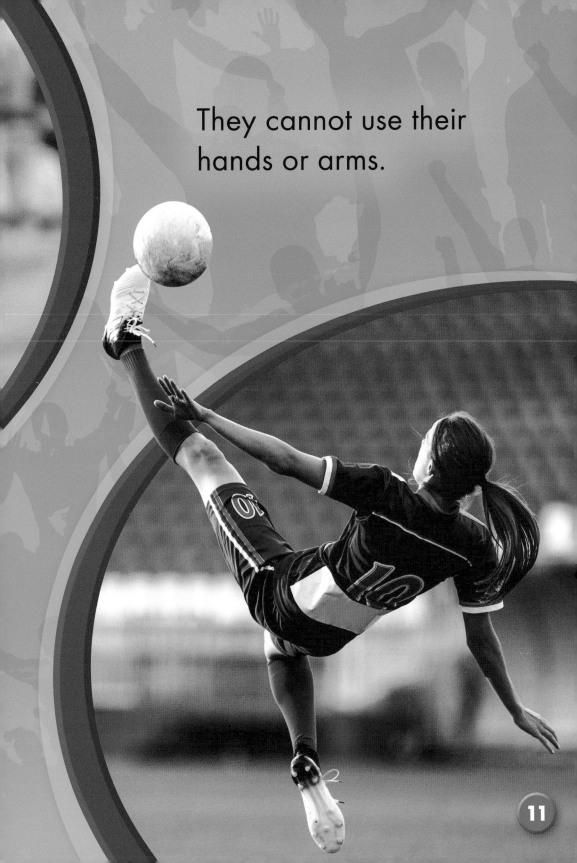

Midfielders are good at passing. They pass the ball to the **forwards**.

Forwards have great foot skills.
They score the most goals!

defender

Defenders help the goalie guard the goal.

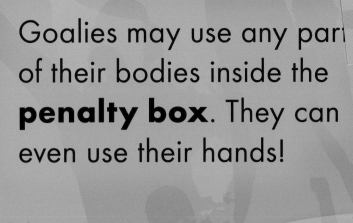

Goalies may use any part of their bodies inside the **penalty box**. They can even use their hands!

15

Sometimes players can safely **tackle** to get the ball. But they cannot trip or push.

tackle

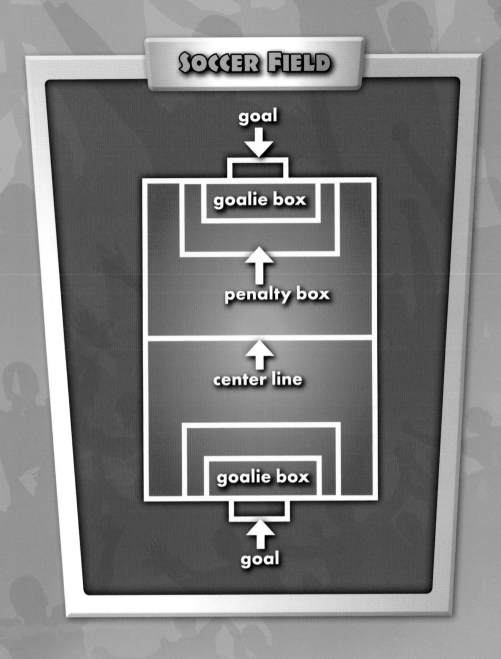

SOCCER FIELD

goal

goalie box

penalty box

center line

goalie box

goal

Players who get tripped or pushed take a **penalty kick**.

Soccer players wear shin guards. These pads keep their lower legs from getting hurt.

Soccer Gear

soccer ball

shin guards

cleats

Shoes with **cleats** help players run on the grassy field.

Soccer players wear lightweight jerseys and shorts. Goalies wear gloves to help catch the ball.

The goalie dives for the ball. What a save!

Glossary

cleats—bumps on the bottom of soccer shoes to help players run on the field

defenders—players who try to keep the other team from scoring

forwards—players who play in attacking positions and try to score goals

goal—an area where a ball is kicked in to score points in a soccer game

goalie—the player who guards the goal to keep the other team from scoring

midfielders—players who play near the middle of the field and try to get the ball to the forwards

penalty box—the large rectangle in front of each goal; goalies can use any part of their bodies to block the ball in the penalty box.

penalty kick—a free shot on the goal, with only the goalie there to try to stop the ball

tackle—to try to take the ball from another player

trap—to stop the ball and control it

To Learn More

Bugler, Beth, and Mark Bechtel. *My First Book of Soccer*. New York, N.Y.: Liberty Street, 2017.

Rebman, Nick. *Soccer*. Lake Elmo, Minn.: Focus Readers, 2019.

Sherman, Jill. *Hockey*. Minneapolis, Minn.: Bellwether Media, 2020.

ON THE WEB

FACTSURFER

Factsurfer.com gives you a safe, fun way to find more information.

1. Go to www.factsurfer.com.

2. Enter "soccer" into the search box and click 🔍.

3. Select your book cover to see a list of related web sites.

Glossary